Ladies Please!
Raise Your Daughters Right

Misplaced Identity

by

Jeanette Murphy

authorHOUSE®

AuthorHouse™
1663 Liberty Drive, Suite 200
Bloomington, IN 47403
www.authorhouse.com
Phone: 1-800-839-8640

First published by AuthorHouse 11/22/2008

ISBN: 978-1-4343-7812-5 (sc)

Printed in the United States of America
Bloomington, Indiana

This book is printed on acid-free paper.

Acknowledgments

Holy Spirit I acknowledge you alone for all you have done in my life. You are my strength, helper, counselor, comforter, and best friend. To my niece, Jeanelle; my brother, Melvin Jr.; my sister, Priscilla; and our special little friends, O'neal, Marquise, Kenneth, Danny, Enetria, Gerard and Nico; my sister Lorraine, my sister Kelly and her three children, Quintin, Terrence, and Kyron. I would not be living today if you had not stepped into my life. Special thanks to JNP, IA, DK and AB.

Contents

Momma's Little Girl

Today you found out that you are pregnant whether planned or not or married or not. The reality is you have a little person growing inside of you who has now become one of your primary responsibilities. As a mom it is your job to nurture and provide a safe, warm, loving environment for your baby. This is important because it will determine how productive he or she will be as an adult. If the baby is surrounded by love and acceptance, they will spring forth into a confident individual and touch many lives. On the other hand, if the baby is raised in a negative, unloving environment, it's possible he or she will grow up and substitute parental care for gangs or multiple partners. Finding themselves embracing a host of false support systems because Mom or Dad was not available or was not concerned. I'm starting to wonder if mothers really are investing in their babies' lives? Are they really spending quality time with them? I believe we have placed so much emphasis on feeding, sheltering and providing that we left out nurturing not understanding the baby wants to talk, play, cuddle and be held in a set of warm loving arms. Babies want daily interaction from you, not wind-up toys or stuffed animals. They want your affection and attention. Remember you are the first example in this new life what you say and do as they grow up will either encourage or discourage them. When I am out shopping or running errands, I see many young girls fussing, cussing, pushing on their small children in public and telling them how dumb they are every time they did something wrong. Why are you diminishing your child's self-worth and confidence before they can begin to think or decide for themselves? I know you're probably thinking they are too young and will not remember what was said, I beg to differ. Consider visiting a local youth correctional facility where females are housed and strike up a conversation with one of them. They will tell you how their mother used profane language toward them and spoke down to them like an animal instead of a human being. Words are powerful and effective. They alter our thinking and our moods, which generally control our actions. Please don't allow your words to add to the many causes of suicide among young people. Keep your mouth away from your children if you're not going to affirm them. They do not deserve your attitude remember you are the adult. You want to build them up while they are young, not tear them down. Some parents need a time out moment before they speak to their children to keep from damaging their spirit. Life is going to deal them enough blows and leave behind several scars without your help. I'm not telling you how to parent; I'm suggesting a different approach than the norm. I know it gets a little rough sometimes hang in there and keep praying until something happens. This is why one should think twice before having babies. In my mind I can hear someone asking what cost is there? Well, one of many costs is your freedom to come and go as you please. The second cost is financial, and the third, most expensive cost is you. You're not your only focus anymore, your baby is. Haven't you noticed a lot of things you did when you were without child you are not available to do anymore? Things have changed for you whether you accept it or not. For some women having a child does not change their program no matter what. They will leave their child with anyone at the drop of a dime. I believe we need to keep reminding young women how hard it is to take care of a baby out of wedlock. Why toil alone when you could have a permanent help mate at your disposal if you wait for marriage? When are you going to get tired of that live-in lover who helps out occasionally when he can be found? Everyone needs help raising a child in this day and age. Yes, I know some women can and do raise their children alone and this is great. However, the load would be much lighter if you had some assistance in the home. In case you forgot, the school system, friends, grandparents, or any other relatives are not responsible for your child. You laid down and did the birthing. You applied for this life time job with consent now handle your business. Life is hard enough as it is keeping you together now you have to assist in developing a baby which requires a lot of attention and patience. So gird up your mind because you are about to get stretched mentally and emotionally like never before. Your world is now her world along with the tears and fears you will experience on this journey. No matter the path you have to take, never give up. Continue pouring into her life and spending time with her. As your child gets older it's not the huge, spectacular things you did for her she will tell others about. It's the small and simple "thank you for spending time with me" things she will hold dear to her heart. Do the tea cup and dish thing at her table and watch some children's programs together. Read her a book while she's resting in your arms. Do things together so she can get to know you and you can get to know her. She needs more from you than your title or friendship she needs a nurtured life. Without this there is a fifty percent chance as she grows up she will end up uneducated with a child out of wedlock, addicted to sex or strung out on some type of drug. Why would a loving mother want her daughter to experience these things? Do you not love her enough to prevent this from happening? I am convinced that neglect and a lack of guidance produce welfare recipients, degrading video dancers, strippers, and prostitutes. If you don't pour any morals or values into your child, you'll get nothing in return. I think adults forget that children come into the world clueless and are totally dependent on someone to steer them in the right direction. They understand nothing, having been stretching, moving, and living inside of the womb for nine months (fewer for some). Is it not clear that your child needs you to survive? If she needed you to feed her through the umbilical cord then, she certainly needs you all the more once she has been born. I believe insecure women who have low self-esteem were deprived of attention at an early age. Could this be the reason why some girls grow up into petty individuals who whine all the time and cannot stand on their own two feet? Ladies, please do your job and raise your daughters right. Abandoning them physically and psychologically is not an option anymore. If you cannot afford to take care of the young person you are birthing, practice abstinence or use some form of protection. It's not fair to this child, who did not ask to be born, to enter into an unprepared environment. I know this sounds a bit old-fashioned, but whatever happened to a home where both parents (married) would agree on when to have a child? Today, if a couple is living together in the same household and is unmarried, they produce kids like there is no tomorrow. Do you not care how your child is viewing this? As the child grows up, he or she will think this is normal when indeed it's not. Do not write me or e-mail me if you disagree; this is my opinion only. Let me stretch your imagination for a second. Could it be the world is in a horrible state due to single-family homes or homes with both parents putting in long hours at work? If everyone is working, who's doing the nurturing? Children need more than provision. They need to be loved and trained with a firm hand. Too often we are leaving them alone to raise them self. This is dangerous and unwise, what do they know? We're letting video games and music inject ideas into their mind and wonder why they stray and become rebellious. Mom, as your little girl grows up she needs to spend majority of her time with you, not the television or her friends. It's your image she needs to capture and hold on to. She needs your instructions on how a lady should conduct herself.

When I was a child, my mother did not spend quality time with me. Her not doing so opened the door for my undeveloped mind to absorb misinformation and bring harm into my life. Yes, I turned out okay; however, I made a lot of mistakes that almost cost me a future. For example, along the way I developed a drinking habit, a smoking habit, and other unhealthy habits at a young age I did not plan. More than ever it's time to pay close attention to your daughters. It's also time to make better choices regarding the mates we are selecting as well. Yes, I know no one is perfect; I hear this all the time. However, you want a mature mate around to help shape your child's life. How in the ham-and-cheese can an unstable husband or significant other help shape your daughter's life? What comic books are you reading to help you choose a decent mate? Are you deciding based on his muscular physique, handsome looks, and how well he can float your boat? You need more than a piece of eye candy. You need a stable, loving and caring individual around your daughters. Stop letting anyone into your child's life just because they might have a lot to offer or material possessions to give. This means nothing if the person rapes or molests your child without your knowledge. This is why it's important that you are around; otherwise someone will strip your child of their innocence at a young age. There's more to raising children than what we think. Are you sure this is what you want? Are you ready for the demands and requirements? Are you emotionally sound to take on this job? Not changing the subject, how in the world are you dressing your daughters? I don't ever recall wearing clothes with my midsection showing or a little makeup on my face with an adult hairstyle like I see today. As I was driving into work one Tuesday afternoon, a mother was crossing the street with her children. As they were walking in front of my car, I noticed the daughter was wearing makeup with a hair style beyond her age. She looked very young and was dressed like a fifteen-year-old high school student although she was only about eight or nine. I am not saying all mothers allow this way of dressing; however, you see it almost everywhere. This is not acceptable, nor is it cute. It causes curiosity to surface in the minds of perverted sex offenders and relatives who have no problem sleeping with someone in the family. You are placing your child in harm's way based on the clothing you are purchasing for them. Your daughter does not have to dress like everyone else. For God's sake, she is a child! Why are you teaching her at an early age the need to feel accepted by her peers? Did you have this problem? I thought you were supposed to teach her how to be herself and not to go along with what everyone else is doing? I guess when she's older and her schoolmates decide to get high or skip school and she follows along, is this okay with you? Ladies, teach and guide your daughters. If you do this, she will not follow the in crowd and rebel against you. I know some mothers do invest in their daughter's upbringing, and this is to be commended. Society thanks you so much for your participation. However, some of us are not doing this, and it's creating problems in the world. When discipline is administered properly, unplanned pregnancy, early jail and cemetery visits will cease. With all your might ladies try and prevent your daughters from becoming another statistic to society. I am begging you: please, raise her right. Be visible and active in her life and let her know how much you love her. Remember she is a replica of you and how you were raised. Either you will smile upon her or frown, you choose.

SPIRITUAL NUGGETS

The book of Psalms 127:3 page 856 (NLT) Holy Bible, "People's Parallel Edition," Tyndale 1997.

Children are a gift from the Lord: they are a reward from Him.

The book of Proverbs 22:6 page 891 (NLT) Holy Bible, "People's Parallel Edition," Tyndale 1997.

Train up a child in the way he should go; and when he is old, he will not depart from it.

The book of Matthew 19:14 page 1280 (NLT) Holy Bible, "People's Parallel Edition," Tyndale 1997.

But Jesus said, Let the children come to me. Don't stop them for the Kingdom of Heaven belongs to such as these.

Resources

Boys/Girls Club of America: (800) 854-CLUB

Big Brothers and Sisters of Greater L.A.: (800) 207-7567

Girls Scouts of USA: (800) 478-7248
Info@gogirlsonly.org

Teenage Hype

From bottles, diapers, and clinging to your legs when you leave her presence, your dependent daughter is becoming independent of you. She is starting to explore, form opinions, collect habits, and struggle with curiosity and rebellion at the same time. Don't be alarmed. She is trying to locate her identity while a transition is taking place, changing her from a little girl into a teenager. Everything around her and inside of her is starting to change, including her relationship with you, her siblings, and neighborhood friends. Her focus has now shifted from home to school now that she has gotten older. She is being introduced to new ideas and concepts without your approval. This is why guidance and stability are needed in the beginning stages of her life. All of a sudden she wants to know why some girls at school are more developed and prettier than others, and why all the guys like those kinds of girls. She looks at boys and wonders how is it some are drop-dead gorgeous and fit and some are just plain looking and not worth her time? Along the way she will discover everything that glitters is not gold as she continues to grow and check the boys out. She has yet to understand looks can be deceiving and talk is cheap. Beep! Beep! News flash: Mom, sex has already creped its way into the forefront of her mind. She has become interested in both genders. No, she is not confused about her sexuality. She is just wondering why the attention is coming from both sides. If she has self-esteem issues and lacks guidance, she will give into these advances and possibly lose her virginity. If you were to conduct a poll around the world, how many virgins do you think you would find? Not many, I'm sure, because there were no disciplinarians in the home. So what do we expect? I know parents do their best in communicating and trying to raise their children. And I also know teenagers have their own minds and will flip out on their parents in a second. Everything we do in life is a risk; no less when it comes to parenting as well. When I was a teenager, I tried to grow up way too fast. I started hanging around the wrong crowd, ditching school, having sex and lost sight of myself as I tried to fit in.

What a waste of valuable time on my part. I had no clue my life and friendships would change over a short period of time. I say all this to convey: put on the having-sex brakes especially if you are not going to marry the person you handed your under garments to. If the truth be told most boys are out to hit it and quit it. Before you know it, you'll look up and they're gone. Now you are left with a child or an unwanted pregnancy. Why spread yourself thin emotionally at such a young age? Now do you see why a mother's influence is so important? It's important because of teenage pregnancy and sexually transmitted diseases. I am reminded of the friends I hung out with in Junior High School when I was twelve years old. During lunch and PE class the only thing we basically had on our minds was the next popular hangout spot or who was doing whom. I'm sorry to say our education was not important to us at the time. Those tall, fine-looking athletes were. If anyone wanted to get with us they had to be a basketball or football player. Anyone outside of these two sports was not important to us or worth our time. I believe my life has been extended to tell young girls you can be about the boys and get an education at the same time. Just don't lose your mind or your virginity in the process. I might have been a little wild in school and hung out with the wrong crowd. However, I was not trying to get down with everybody. Lucky for me, it was not about how many boys I could get with or what I needed to do to become popular. I did not have that problem like most girls do today. This is why it's very important for a young girl to know who she is and what she want out of life. If she stays focused on school work, her mind will be stable and she will excel in all her classes. If she hangs out with no goals to reach for, her mind will wander into trouble. Ladies, stay on your daughter's trail and make sure you tell her about the boys. Don't fool yourself she needs to know their role or she will fall prey to the manipulation and sexual advances from them. This is how a positive father figure can protect her. If his values are in place, he can train her on what qualities to look for in a young man as she prepares for the dating scene. This will prevent young boys from using her mind or her body. Life is difficult enough as it is with peer, performance, acceptance, physical, social, and emotional pressures surrounding her. Teach her how to hold on to who she is and out last these pitfalls. I cannot imagine the struggles teenagers face daily without having someone around to listen and guide them. They need instruction from someone who understands what they are going through. Ladies, listen to your daughter's concerns and monitor her relationships closely. Don't shut her out or she will lean into his arms and confuse sex for love and concern. Also don't be afraid to discipline (not abuse) her when correction is needed. Without correction, unplanned pregnancy, dropping out of school, substance abuse, suicide, promiscuity and staying out late, and disrespecting adults is knocking at her door. Bless my mother's heart, she did the best she could in raising her four daughters. However, we needed more than, "Don't do this or that"— and all the threats of taking away our privileges or having to stay in the house for a number of weeks when we disobeyed. Our first need was for mom to show us who we were. We needed support and directions not go to your room. Interact with your daughter and let her watch how you do things around the house. Teach her how to cook, keep the house in order, wash laundry, manage money, pay bills, choose good friends, and govern her life. I was not taught these things. I was too busy chasing the boys and stuck on self. This is why I constantly say, throughout this book, how much your daughter needs your guidance. If you chose not to make yourself available in her life, the world will. It will suck her in and teach her instant gratification in exchange for her soul. It will teach her how important looks are and that sleeping around can get her anything in life. Ladies, get in your daughter's business and find out what she is doing. Start getting involved in every area of her life <u>not controlling</u> but involved. I think you have forgotten her mind has changed since the little-girl stage. She is now a teenager who requires more attention and advanced training. She needs to be strengthened in the areas of trust, accountability, responsibility, time management, and how to respect adults. I believe this is the stage parents are skipping. All minds change just like school, no one stays in the first grade his/her entire life. The mind is the same way: it is developing all the time, just like your daughter is. Work closely with her; find out what she is passionate about and guide her in that direction. If she is happy, she will stay focused and determined. Keep reminding her not to waste time doing nothing with people who obviously are showing by the way they hang out they have no plans for their future. Don't get me wrong; I am not saying you cannot hang out. What I am saying is mothers know what is best and you need balance. When I was young, I thought my mother was crazy. She always wanted to tell me what to do and how to do it, and at times she gave me no breathing space. She would not let me hang out or date. I would say, "My friends mothers let them stay out late and date. Why do I have a curfew and can't date boys?" She would become silent and tell me to go ask my father. Now, girls, you know how some fathers are when it comes down to their little girls with boys and staying out late at night. The first thing on his mind is, "my little girl is not going to get pregnant by anyone, she needs to stay focused on her education." Today I understand, yet I snuck around and did what I wanted too under my mother's roof, anyway. I lied about staying overnight at a girlfriend's house when I actually sneaked out and went on a date with a guy or attended a party. That's old news your mother or father may have did the same thing. The problem is they never shared it with you. It's time to be honest with your daughters about yourself and your life as a teenager. If you continue withholding information, the world will damage her thinking and cause her to make wrong choices with no concern for her future. I love to see a young girl with her life together. It makes me happy inside because I desired the same thing at her age. If you are a teen who happened to have birthed a child out of wedlock, you can still turn your life around for the better. Don't let this keep you from dreaming of a bright future. Press past this setback. It's not a mistake you just got off the course. There are far too many mothers who do not hang in there and see their daughters through situations like this. It's not the end of the world. Help her pick up the pieces and get moving again. Put your loving arms around her and do some encouraging. Talk to her and tell her all things are still possible, if only she can believe in herself. Help is available, as I always say, upon request. Learn to listen and obey your mothers and make them proud of you. Mothers, love your daughters. Daughters embrace your mothers' advice.

SPIRITUAL NUGGETS

The book of Proverbs 1:8-9 page 531, (NLT) Holy Bible New Living Translation Metal Edition, Tyndale 1996.

Listen my child, to what your father teaches you. Don't neglect your mother's teaching. What you learn from them will crown you with grace and clothe you with honor.

The book of Ephesians 6:1-2 page 957, (NLT) Holy Bible New Living Translation Metal Edition, Tyndale 1996.

Children, obey your parents because you belong to the Lord, for this is the right thing to do. "Honor your father and mother." This is the first of the Ten Commandments that end with a promise. And the promise: If you honor your father and mother, "you will live a long life, full of blessings."

The book of 1 Thessalonians 4:3 page 1569, (KJV) Holy Bible "People's Parellel Edition," Tyndale 1997.

For this is the will of God, even your sanctification, that ye should abstain from fornication.

The book of Ecclesiastes 12:1 page 912, Holy Bible "People's Parallel Edition," Tyndale 1997.

Don't let the excitement of your youth cause you to forget your Creator.

The book of Proverbs 15:5 page 883-884, Holy Bible "People's Parallel Edition," Tyndale 1997.

Only a fool despises a parent's discipline; whoever learns from correction is wise.

Resources

Big Brothers and Big Sisters Club: (215) 567-7000

Youth Crises Line: (800) 843-5200

Suicide National (US) Hotline: (800) SUICIDE

Sexual Transmitted Diseases National Hotline: (800) 227-8922

National (US) Runaway Switch Board: (800) 621-4000

Eating Disorder Awareness and Prevention: (800) 931-2237

Alcohol and Drug Helpline: (800) 821-4357

Young Adult

Having survived the crazy teenaged stage with a few bumps and bruises, your daughter is now on her way into becoming the confident young adult all mothers dream of and want their daughters to be. Not arrogant but confident there is a difference. Arrogance is born of this world centered on pride. Confidence is born out of love and training from the heart of a mother who is concerned about her daughter. Because you took the time to properly raise her she knows exactly what she wants out of life. She's not wasting time chasing men, running from club to club, or hanging out late at night spending your money going no where. She's focused on her future and her life is in order. Unfortunately not all young ladies can say this about their life. Many of them were not nurtured or instructed at a young age. Their parents were too busy earning a living or trying to keep up with the neighbors. Disagreeing with this statement is allowed only if you worked hard and sacrificed for a college education or purchased a home for the family. If not, you should be ashamed of yourself. What could have been more valuable than your daughter's development? I hope you did not place making more money and trying to impress people above your child's welfare. We all need money to survive but what about the children? Who is preparing them on how to navigate through this crazy world? When you do not participate in your child's life you are producing a possible inmate, prostitute, drug addict or gang member. If setting and reaching goals is not the primary focus in their life crashing parties, having sex, drinking and getting high will be. I know young people think this way of living is the life however, it is a destructive irresponsible behavior. Look at the evidence surrounding us today young people behaving badly with or without parental consent. I know this is your life and you can do whatever you want with it. Just don't waste it you've only been giving one. You are not a cat so don't worry about the nine lives people think they really are given. I'm not fussing; I am angry because women are a gift to the world. We have the opportunity to birth and raise a human being into a wonderful person and we're falling short of this and to top it off, we are not being respected. I know everyone has issues I understand that; however, we can at least put some at bay. Has anyone ever told you that you are your worst enemy? It's not the person or problem on the outside that's creating havoc. Ninety-nine percent of the time, it's you and the decisions that are being made. When are we going to realize not everything wrong with us is generational some things are learned. We are inflicting ourselves and blaming everyone including the cat and the goldfish for our problems. I'm bringing these concerns to the surface so you can think about them and make some changes and we can begin to produce productive human beings in society. No matter what's going on in your life you are not alone; even the highly educated and the rich have problems and issues. Stop making up excuses because of your childhood, or if you were an orphan or abused. You can still make a change for the better. I sympathize with you one hundred percent, and your wounded upbringing does pain my heart. However, if you plan to recover from your past, you need to begin taking a few steps. The first step you need to take is to surround yourself with positive influences. Second, you must gather some courage. If Mom is not available, I am sure there are other relatives who are successful (not rich) within your reach. Help is present, so get up and dust yourself off. It's tough and scary, I know however, it can be done. I am a witness I had to leave some friends, get alone with God, and straighten out my life in order to see what was ahead. When I did this, God helped me discover a hidden passion of mine. I rediscovered my love for poetry, writing, and helping people pick their lives up and giving them ideas on how to better their value in society. I don't know everything, however, I have been living for forty something years now, so I am qualified to say something. In reference to this book, one of my co-workers said to me, "You don't have any children, how can you tell someone how to raise their daughter?" Good question. What Mr. J.K. Perez failed to realize is that I was once a little girl and a teenager. Today, with a smile on my face, I can say I'm becoming the confident woman I am writing about. It took a long time for me to arrive at this place in my life; however, here I am. As I said before, I made many mistakes and caused majority of my own pain. People took the very words I shared and exchanged them for weapons against me. It's not always wise to be open. It's a proclivity that some women have who are over friendly. We rarely take a step back and observe our relationships with people. We have got to learn how to guard our hearts and stop falling for the okie dokie whether the person is a male or female. If you have been hurt by someone who stripped you of a future rise up out of those ashes. Shake off the disappointments, regrets and rejections. All things are still possible no matter what has occurred in your life. I know someone who can help you if no one else can. His name is **JESUS**. He will lift you above whatever situation you may be facing. He will strengthen you and set you back on the right path on your own two feet, with power. When I was in my early twenties or was it thirties? I had no positive influences in my circle. If I did, I was too stiff necked to recognize it. I figured I was grown I worked and I brought home my own bacon. I was the one getting up every morning, working eight hours a day, so when I got off work, it was party time. I had no problem having fun as long as I was living at home and not being a responsible person. To my surprise, I received a knock on the door of my life from Responsibility and Accountability when I left my parents home. Long story short, I ended up making a mess out of my life because no one prepared me for the young-adult role. I had no idea there was more to life than hanging out. I lost track of time, myself, and my future. At this stage in my life, my issues and errors were starting to surface and grab my attention, requiring solutions for which I had none. I wasted years chasing after nothing that I thought meant everything. Like many other women, my life appeared to be exciting when in reality it was empty and unfulfilling. I existed with no life line flowing through my veins to say the least. I was unhappy and all the material things I gained over a period of time did not change things one bit. My story is just one of many, there are other women who can tell you how they were damaged severely and required years of therapy or a strong, patient, and loving individual to come into their life and turn things around. I believe love is the only antidote that can be applied to a broken life and bring healing. If we can do this for each other, we can change the world one person at a time. Sometimes being broken can help redirect our paths in life because some of us are going the wrong way. Could it be some young women are jailed because it's the safest place for them since they're not in the business of wanting to change? No one but God knows. Wow! I've talked so much about my own personal pain I forgot what I was talking about. Oh! Getting back to the life of young girls I see on a daily basis. I see many of them with children I believe were unplanned. They looked tired, worn down, and depressed. Life would have offered opportunities to them if they had waited to have children. When we have children out of order, it causes extra stress in our lives that we do not need, because we are no longer providing for our self anymore. We now have extra mouths to feed along with new pressures to deal with. This is why we sometimes see mothers hitting and slapping these little people who are not old enough to defend themselves.

They did not ask to be born; they arrived on the scene involuntarily. Also, I see you girls with men who are old enough to be their fathers. I thought to myself over a period of time, did these girls have a positive male image in their life? Could this be why they are dating this substitute father? I believe our little girls are drawn to these older men because they are seeking support, protection, security, and love they did not receive from their father because he was absent or did not present these qualities to them. Others have concluded in their mind these young girls are looking to cash in or receive material possessions from these gentlemen. I'm sorry to burst your bubbles; it's a lot deeper than this. There was never a father-daughter relationship in her life. Last and certainly not least, I would like to discuss how young girls who are not raised properly are out on the street selling their bodies for drugs. Some are homeless and some come out during the day or late at night to make money to pay for what they want. They want quick money and not a nine-to-five-job like everyone else. I am certain if these young women were in the correct state of mind, they would not be selling their bodies. They would be working or in school, learning a trade or skill. I know it breaks their mother's heart to see her daughter on the street, living a life she could never imagine. Where there is no discipline with a loving hand there are sad consequences. Today many young people do not want to start from the bottom of the barrel. They refuse to accept minimum-wage jobs. They want instant success and fast money. Can you hear Wisdom crying out, "show them the way and point them to the truth about obtaining quick riches." Inform them it's okay to wait, struggle, and do without to get what they want in life, this builds character. There is a process of growth that needs to take place. Without this process like many stars in Hollywood you will end up making a mess of your life. How many times have you turned on your television to find out another movie stars or well known person reach a place of honor or fame and lost it shortly thereafter because of a lack of character? Having a gift or talent may get you through a door; however, character will keep you there permanently. Mothers, I cannot stress this enough: it's very important how you raise your daughters. We are the womb carriers and get first shot at the development process before any school or program. Continue informing her even at this age because she still needs your guidance. Girls, we can never be to grown to receive advice from our loving mothers. Today, my mother is no long with me and I miss her with all my heart. No I did not take in all of her advice (I wish I did) however, what I did not do I hope you will so you can have a wonderful life early on.

SPIRITUAL NUGGETS

The book of 1 Corinthians 7:34, page 1511, (KJV) Holy Bible "People's Parallel Edition," Tyndale 1997.

There is a difference also between a wife and a virgin. The unmarried woman careth for the things of the Lord, that she may be holy both in body and spirit.

The book of Romans 12:1-2, page 1496, (NLT) Holy Bible "People's Parallel Edition," Tyndale 1997.

And so, dear brothers and sisters, I plead with you to give your bodies to God. Let them be a living and holy sacrifice the kind he will accept. When I think of what he has done for you, is it too much to ask? Don't copy the behavior and customs of this world but let God transform you into a new person by changing the way you think. Then you will know what God wants you to do, and you will know how good and pleasing and perfect his way really is.

Resources

Mentors peer resources: www.mentors.ca/askamentor.
html

Girls Inc. (Central Coast): (800) 374-4475

Youth Opportunities United: (513) 961-2000

Sophisticated Lady

Finally having gained a little wisdom through trial and error, this thirty-year-old smart, strong, and sophisticated lady is strutting victoriously through life at the beat of her own drum. She has gleaned all she needs to make this next transition into adulthood smooth. The morals and values she has held on to speak volumes everywhere she goes. When she walks into a crowded room, the very essence of who she has developed into turns the heads of many. Her demeanor and appearance announces, "I am a well developed female and will not settle for less." There is no need to dress for attention or to impress anyone. I am positive, approachable, friendly and I govern myself accordingly. I am on top of my game and I lack or owe nothing. No matter where I go, I make a difference in the lives of others whether at work, home, or play. There is no limit to what I can do or who I can become, because of the love I received at a young age. Keep in mind; this is the ideal sophisticated lady. In fact, there are many women who do not fall into this category. I'm not putting anyone down, just keeping it on the straight and narrow. They are trying to keep up with the hype and exchanging sex for another material possession. They play mind games with everyone they come in contact with just to get what they want. In other words, misuse and deplete is her first and last name and what she plans to do to you if you allow it. Instead of planning her future, she's too busy trying to be down with everyone making sure she has the latest Chanel apparel or the hottest Coach, Louis Vuitton, Prada, Jimmy Choo, Christian Louboutin, and so on; clothing, shoes, or handbags. It's okay to have these things don't get me wrong. Just don't let this force you to prostitute yourself since you're trying so hard to keep up with the Johnsons and the Joneses. Stop spending other folk's money and start focusing on getting your life in order. If you don't curb this habit there's a chance of rain approaching the horizon and you are headed for a disaster. Either you will go back home to Momma, live off some friends here and there, or end up in a mission because you did not have the means to survive your expensive spending habit. You have been living life based on how the world says you should live instead of how your mother may have been trying to teach you since you were a little girl. You have no character and you lack self control. All you know is how to take and give nothing in return. You are indecisive and you never complete what you set out to accomplish. You are messy and insecure and are always involved in other folks' business. How can you achieve any goals? You are too busy. Get a life! Start doing what it takes and begin to make something happen for you. This is not a put-down it's a self-examination moment, because at this stage in life, there should be some kind of order not more victims or plots. Unfortunately, as adults, sometimes we never grow out of our childish tendencies. Our bodies are mature by nature; however, we lack character therefore making life hard. Ladies, an adult is a person who has arrived at maturity in size and strength. Our age does not make us mature it's only a number. So don't get it twisted because a lot of grown people have more game than Nintendo does. It's going to take more than a beautiful face and tight body to make it in this life. We are going to need some character, intelligence, and an education. Does anyone want to be their best in life anymore by using their brain instead of their beauty? Stop letting this world system continue influencing your thoughts and behavior through television and music.

These tools are sending conflicting messages to our young women at and early age by thinking riches will give you a significant place in this world. I'm not saying you cannot view television, dvds or listen to music. All I am saying is we need balance. Too much time was spent on being the cat's meow, instead of focusing on life and accomplishing goals. Stop procrastinating get up and make something happen. There are many resources out there to enhance your life. Pick up the telephone and make some calls, search the Internet, or go to your local library for assistance. Begin to look into different schools and companies for trade and skill-enhancing programs. Everyone possesses a valuable and useful treasure inside of them. Start digging and discover your destiny. If you are a great cook, consider becoming a mobile caterer or open up your own restaurant. If you are handling your business at home, raising children, then open up your own childcare center. If you can sew your kid's clothes, then become an at home seamstress or create your own clothing website. If you can decorate your house, then become a decorator. If you can help people solve their problems and you're good at it, think about going back to school to become a therapist or a counselor. Get alone and find out what you are passionate about. Then begin to develop and get going. Last yet very important, I want to talk about marital relationships. A real man wants a real woman in his life. I am not talking about a person who wears makeup, dresses, heels and carries a purse. I am talking about the female who knows who she is and does not drain the life out of her man because she lacks an identity. She is not paging him 24/7 or having her girls spy on him or going through his things looking for phone numbers. Look closer ladies, he already has his life together and his identity intact. He is solid and secure with his manhood. He is not running around town with several different women; he knows exactly what he wants. If you want a good man make sure you get yourself together and stop trying to be his mother, ordering him around and giving him a critical attitude. Do you know how much pressure men are under in this world today? They are always performing just to be accepted on the job, in the family, and among friends. It's almost like they have to prove they are real men just to exist. When your man is with you, he does not want any demands placed on him. He wants your love, and acceptance. He wants to know that you are concerned about him by asking how his day was. Make him feel good about being your main squeeze. Always keep the communication lines open so he will not think life is centered on you and your struggles alone. Let him know that he is essential in this relationship if not the other woman will. She will listen to everything in his mind and before you know it your man has another chick on the side. If you are not going to cater to him why commit yourself to him? Make yourself available and do not give him a reason to look outside of your relationship. Don't drain your man's emotions, ladies. Learn to handle some things on your own. He has a lot on his plate, so be the help mate that he needs. Stop nagging him; embrace and love on him. At any rate, by any means necessary, take a step outside of your comfort zone and become that sophisticated lady the world and all men are waiting and looking for.

SPIRITUAL NUGGETS

The book of 1 Peter 3:3, page 1618 (NLT) Holy Bible "People's Parallel Edition."

Don't be concerned about the outward beauty that depends on fancy hair styles, expensive jewelry, or beautiful clothes, you should be known for the beauty that comes from within, the unfading beauty of a gentle and quiet spirit, which is so precious to God.

The book of Proverbs 16:21, page 885, (KJV) Holy Bible "People's Parallel Edition," Tyndale 1997.

The wise in heart shall be called prudent: and the sweetness of her lips increaseth learning.

Resources

www.retreatsconnection.com

Hi Point Women Center, Inc.: (937) 592-7734

Essence Communication Inc. (212) 522-1212

Verizon Foundation: (800) 360-7955

Virtuous Woman

Who can find a virtuous woman with inner beauty in this modern day society who conducts herself like a real lady? Whose value supersedes a flawless diamond. Whose life is centered and set on glorifying God; honoring her husband, nurturing the children, working and keeping her home in order. Ladies, are we prepping our little girls with any virtue today? Are we trying to establish any principles in place while they are young? Why does it appear as if the majority of them have grown into women who disrespect their husbands, neglect his needs, has a problem being the weaker vessel, and does not have time to keep up the house? How can your husband have any confidence in you when he lays down at night? How does he know without a shadow of a doubt you are going to take care of his children if something was to happen to him? Why are you so brassy? What happened in your life to cause you to take on this "on my terms" attitude? Is there a problem? Is your man not doing his job? Are you encouraging him to be a husband and a father to the children? Stop diminishing him with your words and actions. Your job is to assist and respect him whether you think he deserves it or not. The two of you must form into one union because a house divided cannot stand. With all this said, let's assume this virtuous woman is married. If not, she should be living a chaste, pure, and upright life keeping herself away from anything that might cause her to stumble while living celibate. I know this sound as if it's a hard thing, if you occupy your mind constantly with sexual thoughts, movies, or explicit songs. If you are going to live pure, you must consider thinking about things that have nothing to do with sex. Stop being anxious and learn to wait for what you want. If not you'll keep hooking up with anything or have to share. Stop settling for Mr. Almost Right can't you see he's the wrong person for you? Look at the confusion and unwillingness to make a few adjustments for you. He's not ready for a true relationship with women making it easy for him to cheat by saying yes to his advances instead of no. What makes us step outside of our relationships anyway? When will we realize what we have at home is just as good? If you ask me, everyone should take their time selecting a mate so in that one person you can have everything you desire. My man is all that and I am satisfied with him (we're both celibate). I am not looking outside of our relationship for anything new. My eyes are fixed on him, and I do not wander; nor does my body crave or have a taste for anything. I wanted a good man, so I had to work at becoming a good woman. I fought with myself and resisted a lot of temptations, saying no when everything in me wanted to say yes. Men, you say you want a good woman, are you a good man? Are you keeping yourself pure and waiting for Ms. Virtue to arrive on the scene? Or are you out there swinging from every tree that has branches on it? We have got to step back and take a good look at ourselves if we want to be in a good relationship. If you attract men who are crazy, who love having many women, and love spending your money, guess what? He's not the problem, you are. I am not saying all men live like this, so please do not email me, text me, or threaten me. I know we have a few good men out there don't trip. I'm just saying don't be in a hurry and let Mr. Mature work on himself while you work on you! Life has so much to offer, begin to focus on your career and character in the meantime. Maybe down the road the two of you will find each other. Look around you; it's hard to live single and abstinent today. Every time you look up, sex is being advertised from television to print. Does anyone want to hold out anymore? I know you are probably thinking to yourself, why should I not fulfill my physical need just because Mr. Mature is not ready? Well, I can give you two healthy reasons to stay celibate today: AIDS and STDS. This world has gone from being a melting pot into a sex pot. Single and married people alike are having unprotected sex whenever and however. How can we be serious about wanting a one on one relationship when everyone is sneaking around, lying and cheating on each other? Where did this behavior come from to have more than one sexual partner while dating or married? Did our parents not teach us the value of monogamy? I'm not telling anyone how to live their life. I'm warning you how life can be lived so much better without an incurable disease flowing through your body. We have got to stop selling ourselves short and raise the standard high so men can come up a notch if they want to be with us. We need to stop acting and dressing like we are desperate. If you are going to dress to <u>please</u>, instead of dressing to leave a lasting impression, you should expect a man to want your body and not the total you. Before leaving home for school, work, or wherever, check how you are dressed. Just in case you don't, know men play mind games with women who have no problem revealing their jewels (body parts). They normally cater to you based on how you are dressed. If you are a provocative dresser, he wants pleasure from you. If you wear expensive apparel, he might consider dating you, or come after the money he thinks you have. We have got to get beyond looking at the outer appearance and start checking out people's character if we want long term relationships. I would rather have an average looking man who will honor me and treat me like a queen than someone who is fine and disrespectful. I am not saying all men are like this, so don't get upset, but if the shoe fits, slip it on and start walking. I'm not pointing the finger because we all need help being authentic in relationships. Nevertheless, if you are going to date us, be honest upfront and tell us if you are interested in seeing other women. In case you didn't know we get more excited during the dating process than you. We start thinking about how your last name will sound with our kids and our name. We fantasize about the life the two of us can have undisturbed by outside influences. Our mind seriously takes off into wonderland forgetting most of you are players and you lead us on and then drop us like a hot potato. Some of you need to throw away your game cards and leave all the play action up to the NBA and NFL. If you want love, you have to give love in return. With all the millions of people in the world today, what's up with being single? I don't understand it we have seminars, self-help books, Mom or Dad's advice and people still have a problem hooking up. Something is terribly wrong with this picture. Either women are not raising their daughters right or men are not grooming their sons. This cycle will continue if parents do not take the time to nurture and train their children at an early age. What do we expect out of a child once they become an adult if no one placed any value or virtue in them? Why should a man treat a woman right if his parents did not teach him how to and vice versa? I know not everyone was improperly raised and there are some great men and women out there who truly love each other. This is good. Thank you and keep up the good work and maybe you can help others by example. Everyone deserves to be loved by someone. No one wants to be alone their entire life. I am at a wonderful place in my life today, because I have someone who loves and truly cares for me. You have no idea the shaping it took to have these words flowing from my lips. I know life can be fulfilling with or without a mate; however, having one around is a bonus. Sometimes we meet people who do not belong to us; they belong to someone else. This is why I believe some relationships do not work: you have something that does not belong to you. Yes, all relationships are risky because we never know what we are getting involved in, especially when we meet someone for the first time. People will either help you or hurt you anytime you open yourself up to be known and loved. In the meantime work on being a better woman while you are waiting. Go ahead and be that virtuous mother so you can raise a virtuous daughter, and she can raise a virtuous daughter, and so on. The story does not end with you mom. Can you count the number of lives your daughters can touch if you invest in them and prepare them for the future? **<u>Ladies, please raise your daughters right</u>**. And, men, if you happen to grab a copy of this little book, please raise your son's right so they can love and respect our little girls.

Love, Jeanette

SPIRITUAL NUGGETS

The book of Proverbs 3:15, page 872, (KJV) Holy Bible "People's Parallel Edition," Tyndale 1997.

She is more precious then rubies: and all the things thou canst desire are not to be compared unto her.

The book of Proverbs 31:25-26, page 901, (KJV) Holy Bible "People's Parallel Edition," Tyndale 1997.

She is clothed with strength and dignity and she laughs with no fear of the future. When she speaks, her words are wise and kindness is the rule when she gives instructions.

The book of Proverbs 31:17, page 900, (KJV) Holy Bible, "People's Parallel Edition," Tyndale 1997.

She is energetic and strong, and a hard worker.

*Become a mentor.

Heavenly Treasure

There are so many hurting women around the world who have no idea who they are. They are starving for affection and looking in all of the wrong places, trying to fill this void in their lives. Your mother may have birth you, but God made you. And He knows everything about you, even the number of hairs on your head (Matthew 10:30), even if you are missing a few. He knows your uprising and down-setting. He loves you so much He sent His only begotten Son into the world to die for you and free you from destroying yourself. He wants you to trade your selfish desires for His heavenly desires and to give you life in abundance (John 10:10). Does this mean your life will be pain-free? Absolutely not! We live in a troubled world full of sin. However, this heavenly treasure (Jesus) will enable you to handle every problem in life with joy, peace, and strength from Him. If you do not know Jesus as your Savior and Lord, you can receive Him into your life today. First you must confess with your mouth that Jesus is Lord and believe in your heart that God has raised Him from the dead. Then you shall be saved (Romans 10:9). A real miracle is a life changed and transformed by the power and love of God.

Conclusion

adies, once again, life is difficult enough as it is without raising your daughter's right. Why expose her to society without any character or principles in place? Do you want her to end up in jail, prostitute herself on the streets, continue birthing fatherless children, or strung out on drugs? Do you want your daughter to be productive? How about a bright future, a good man, children, and financial stability? Well, raise her correctly. I always hear women complaining about how men don't treat them right or how they disrespect us. The question I will present to you like I did them is, are you a good woman? I'm not talking about your looks, how much money or material assets you have, or whether or not you can cook or are good in bed. A good woman is made by her mother; she has class and character because of the training she received. Mothers, it's your job to come alongside your daughter and work with her while she is in your care. Without guidance, she will let the world defame her person and underestimate her value as a human being. If this happens it will cause her to settle for less in every area of her life. I tell young women all the time there's more to us than clothes, money, makeup, and men. I am not saying all women lives take this route; however, there is a substantial percent that does. I know not all females are sitting back, having babies, with no college education, or seeking sugar daddies to take care of them, or awaiting the death of a parent for an inheritance. I know some of us are attorneys, doctors, directors, real estate agents, optometrists, neurosurgeons, policewomen, senators, executives, division chiefs, entrepreneurs, and so on. The point I am trying to get across is don't settle for less; start reaching for a better life. Let's grow up and stop the cat fighting, gossiping behind each others back, being jealous, and stealing each others man. You are not the cat's meow, and there is always someone out there who looks better and dresses better then you do. As the kids say, "You ain't all that." Why don't we take all of this negative energy we use to hurt each other with and turn that energy into doing something positive for young ladies around the world and locally. Let's start educating, supporting and mentoring. As long as breath is in your body there is hope for you. It's never too late for change or redirection. Trust me; I know how broken you feel, the thoughts of failure you are having, and the regrets that cross your mind time after time. I can feel your tears and the inexpressible words that has been laying dormant in you heart since you were a little girl. I know this pain was expressed through your behavior, your school grades, your appetite, those numerous divorces, and the way you dressed for attention. Yes, you may have been misunderstood and considered a nobody by people who thought they were somebody yet were not important enough to tell you how your future would unfold. Girls, get up, even if you need to shed a few tears or lose some so-called friends. Get up and start over again. If you feel you are too seasoned to start over, reach out and help someone who is less fortunate. Your identity may have been misplaced since childhood and you may have been neglected. However, you are still a lady and your mother's favorite daughter. Once you locate yourself, reach back and help someone else find themself. Let's start loving and lifting each other up. Don't hate participate and learn to be happy for women who are successful and prosperous.

About the Author

Jeanette Murphy is a forty-year-old female born in Shreveport, Louisiana to the parents of Melvin Joe and Gloria Jean, both deceased. The middle child of five presently living in the incredible state of California for the past thirty-eight years. Through many disappointments and setbacks, she has written her first short, to-the-point book called, "*Ladies, Please! Raise Your Daughters Right.*" This book came to fruition based on Jeanette's passion for all mothers to consider raising little girls into productive women not seductive women.